C000025184

Ruth Bidgood
Time Being

seren

Seren is the book imprint of
Poetry Wales Press Ltd.
57 Nolton Street, Bridgend, Wales, CF31 3AE
01656 663018
www.seren-books.com

The right of Ruth Bidgood to be identified as
the author of this work has been asserted in accordance
with the Copyright, Designs and Patents Act, 1988.

© Ruth Bidgood, 2009

ISBN 978-1-85411-491-4

A CIP record for this title is available from the British Library.

All rights reserved. No part of this publication may be reproduced,
stored in a retrieval system, or transmitted at any time or by any means,
electronic, mechanical, photocopying, recording or otherwise without
the prior permission of the copyright holder.

The publisher works with the financial assistance of the Welsh Books Council.

Cover image: photograph of Drygarn Fawr from Cairn, Craig Cnwch by Liz
Fleming-Williams.

Printed in Bembo by Bell & Bain Ltd., Glasgow

£4

Time Being

In memory of my daughter, Janet.
(d. Spring 2007)

Contents

Five Years On

In five years, hardly a thing had changed.
There were pools on the track still,
in the bottom field; after September rain
today's sun and breeze struck sparks
from muddy ripples. After the familiar climb
through oakwoods, the upper valley
made its old spell.
Hedge a bit tidier, perhaps, by the top field,
where the chimneys come into sight.
Almost the same. Almost.

It was as if the chequered years there
had all been halcyon as the day
which now enclosed them; as if
core-samples forced from an arctic seabed
up, up through ice and ice
had grown again their own soft climate,
brought back the lost warm world.

Interviewing

When I was the one with the recorder
I liked the richness of dark and light
in their reminiscing, the unexpectedness,
the shocks and laughter, but not
the drooping voice they used for saying
"All gone now, all over",
or "Water under the bridge, eh?" –
as if there was something wrong
with ending on a high note,
or moving to the present without
that cloying downbeat refrain.

So now when she comes, this likeable girl
with her little gadget, her young hands
(no slack skin, no gravespots) setting it up,
I'm my own censor, ignoring
her questions' invitation
to lament, her disappointed eyes
thirsty for the juice of my tears.

Viewpoint

We parked the Landrover
at a rough turning-place. It had the air
not of an end but a pause
on the way through the forest.
A damp, richly green downward path
(if path it had been) was hopelessly blocked,
trunk after trunk rammed across it
like a clanging-to of bolts.
Hardly more promising, on the other side,
was a mess of boggy ruts, curving down
between banks, losing itself out of sight
below our small circle of clarity.

Feeling beyond the curve might lie
some clue to function, direction,
in the forest's enigmatic design,
we stumbled down, muddily clutching
at grass-tufts on the flanking mounds.
Suddenly, discord breaking
into harmony, we found ourselves
on a green track, surely disused for years,
but walkable, and lower down vanishing
round another curve.

I stood and caught my breath. The other two,
surer-footed, hurried on. At the bend
they stopped, stock still, every line
drawing for me their huge surprise.
Then they started to wave – "Come on!
Come! Look!", and I half-ran
the rest of the way.

The old lane twisted to a shelf of land
that opened on what might have seemed
familiar splendour – a valley we knew,
hills bare, hills forested, and far off,
beyond misty lowlands, a horizon
of true mountains. But from here
we saw it new, aslant, changed,
a beauty of questioning and strangeness.

An hour ago, across the valley,
we'd been on a known slope,
where a pile of stones could rebuild itself
into a house we remembered
from forty years ago; where bridleways
were mapped and understood;
where lines of runaway trees,
once hedgerows, delineated
fields we could trace and name;
where the man at my side
had run as a child, and today
seemed ghosted by that small shadow.

Leaning on the old Landrover
we had looked across at the hill
where now we stood, wondering
why we knew so little of it;
wondering if stones of any house might lurk
in dark of trees; how roads had run;
what meaning might be found in shapes
obscured by veils of forest.

Now in afternoon sun
we drank, delighted, the blend
of known and unknown, of our own
commingled years, of stories told
and stories waiting to be found.
I thought how the end of a life
might be a pause at the top
of a green, ancient road,
where down at the bend loved figures
would turn, amazed, gesturing
"Come! Look! Come!"

Gaps

1. Gaps

This hill-gate is half-hearted
about shutting out or in.
It's more gap than gate, an old
ramshackle something-and-nothing,
with two posts that don't match.
One's a skinny chopped-off pole,
the other a soggy chunk; they hold
two horizontal bars
with a wambling cross between them.

Up here in the wind
the gate's appropriate, a thing
serving a purpose beyond logic, as if
whatever willy-nilly it lets through
was always meant to pass;
like wordless voices
fretting the edge of mind,
half-memories finding a way
through gaps that had to be there.

2. Illusion

After passing the old house
(silent now – stones, moss, tangle)
the path climbs into forest.

These are not voices in the trees,
only sounds like speech
that wind and branches contrive
in the forest's dim arcades.
No-one laughs, no-one cries,
not even that child
whose inconsolable wailing
brings a shiver. Strangest,
more eldritch than any, but real,
comes a goshawk's cry.
Feather and flesh, blood-warm, ravenous
she climbs a tower of air and is gone.

Next month, in troubled weather
of thin high cloud-scud, again
blown trees relay vague words and cries.
One shrill call, surely a goshawk's,
fleshless, bloodless, cold,
caught in the sound-web of illusion
echoes and is gone.

3. Loose Connection

The radio stuttered, crackled, stopped.
Suddenly it spoke again –
                              "Forms of life
that are vast and tenuous,
and drift between the stars..."
Then it died. I scribbled
its terminal vision on a shopping list;
meant to track the programme,
never did.
                Tonight from the hill
I almost see them in the cold sky,
vast forms thinly drifting,
amorphous, dark on dark, alive,
drifting between hard glittering worlds
defined by dead light.

4. From the Parapet

Height, heat, dazzle. Below,
the paved square is assaulted
by ferocious light. Even the fountain
seems not soft flow, but a profligate
hurling of jewels.

Moment by moment,
scores of foreshortened figures,
crossing the square this way or that,
make an infinity of patterns,
each one unique.

It seems worthwhile to stay for a time,
leaning on the parapet, watching,
in case a friend long gone
passes down there, looks up, waves,
goes on walking away.

Local Historian

Facts were his stock-in-trade
and his addiction.
Good to tell name and farm
of the tooth-drawer who pulled
a stubborn molar; better
to add his date of birth,
even the hour and weather
of his first cry. Mapping
his neighbourhood's past,
he couldn't resist the puniest
hillock, quirkiest twist
of a brambly footpath.

When he ordered the carving
of his graduate son's memorial –
the young consumptive
so loved, focus of so much pride –
the austerity of grief
constrained him, enforced
a minimal record: "died at sea,
aged thirty-two".
For once his readers were left
wanting more. There was just one
concession – "buried
in latitude 44.25 North,
longitude 42.10 West" –
to chart the deepest gulf
in an ocean of tears.

Cf. Heaney.

Cart Burial, Young Adult Female

The mound is gone. They have dug down
and found her, angularly folded
on the ghost-shape of a cart,
wheels loosed and scattered.
Beside her, the iron mirror,
smutched with grave-dirt,
is blind to the smashed skull,
the grin of the warped jaw.

"A rare status symbol",
say scholars. Often, perhaps,
she would throw it down,
pettish, dissatisfied
with what it told her,
wanting to be surer
of her power to invite,
her lips' readiness
for kisses to come.

Light pours down
on the hard bed where now she lies,
stretching out her bone arms
for the lovers never to be.

Meeting the Bus

Autumn afternoon dims; one light comes on
up there behind the trees.
By the gate to the farm track
she's waiting for her grandson.
Till the bus comes groaning up the hill
she chats, showing me the field
where the Roman fort stood, and later
a Welsh prince's courthouse.
"I've heard", she says diffidently,
"they say", "I think I've read..."

The yellow bus draws up, children
at the windows, checkng who's meeting who,
holding pictures for us to admire.
The small boy who emerges has a drawing
of a bulbous whale, apparently
in conversation with a caterpillar.

His grandmother points across the road –
"Up that field, near those trees,
was my great-great-grandfather's house".
I do a silent count of generations.
I've known nothing like such rootedness,
can hardly imagine the richness or the bonds.
The child's more interested in a standing stone
against the sky; he thinks it's like a fox,
sitting up to sniff the wind –
and yes, it has a dark and vulpine air.

Going down the hill, I wonder
about ways of belonging; about ties,
making and cutting them; how
of our three generations here
already the young are leaving. A sharp breeze
rumples late roadside honeysuckle.
I feel the tug of those small joining
filaments I've grown,
that tell me I'm no stranger, but placed and known.

Assembling the Pieces

There's a shadowy perch; outside it
a sunlit herringbone
of brick tiles, uneven as if
insecurely covering something.

A panelled door, high-polished,
glows red-brown, but its hasped locks
are dull with rust, look non-negotiable.

A pin-headed stick-man
gleams in pale sharp blue.
He seems fragile, but full
of darting energy.

Is there movement inwards?
The blue man stalks over the tiles
into the porch, makes his stick-hand
an angular fist, thumps the shining panels,
waits for rusty locks to grind open;
waits, and they do.
A black hall swallows him.

Or outwards?
There is a splintering: through jaggedness
a bony blue arm is thrust, stick fingers
wrench at locks, the door swings
creakily open. Out limps the stick-man,
battered, dot-and-carry, just makes it
over the tiles before they tilt and break
this way and that, pushed by the upward thrust
of a tempest of black leaves. He is safe,
he is through, he is doing a limping dance
out, out, his blueness diminishing
against huge blue of sky
over a burgeoning garden.

Lives

The dog dashes away again
down to the river-meadows
and disappears. We can't believe
he's lost, but pause in our snagged passage
along an overgrown path,
and call him in a desultory way.

The valley is full of life,
hardly any of it human.
Big freestanding hawthorns
are coming into bloom;
oaks, ancient vegetable presences,
sport young fern along branches,
pallid fungi on trunks.
To the top of the ridge, firs
climb close and dark. Now and then
a flick, a faint crack, break stillness.

All through the valley, in its mould,
its waters, grasses, old fallen leaves;
under its bark, stones, rushes,
carried on its winds, motes in its sunrays,
are the secret living things,
the valley's nodes and ganglions,
blood-vessels, flesh and bone –
trillions of wings, carapaces,
hairs, feathers, scales,
flakes and films of skin,
horde on horde of scuttling legs,
tiny puffs of breath, and with them
juice of leaf and stem, powder of pollen,
channelled fountaining of sap.

The terrier has found a creature to chase.
We spy him, down the riverbank,
in and out of reed-clumps.
He seems not to notice our calls,
but when we go on, taking a turn
into the trees, he pants and scurries uphill

to follow, being part (when he has to choose)
of our life, not the wild hidden one
he has wallowed in for a while.

We climb out of the valley;
our minds won't lose it.
Minute beings disrupted
by our clearing of wood from the path,
our thrusting back of brambles;
everything crushed by our trampling;
will soon be replaced by the irresistible
fecundity of the place.

Back in his home, the dog
will sleep, twitching.

Clasped Hands

Plodding uphill to the old chapel
I meet her coming down, tugged by the dog
she's walking for her sick brother.
I'm on my way to photograph
clasped hands of stone above a grave;
because the stone is flaking now, and soon
no-one will see how firmly the man's hand
grasps the smaller one, how fingers speak
an interchange of love. "Beloved wife",
says the lettering, "beloved wife". But lichen
is thickening, spreading, and soon Jane's name
and Edward's will be gone.

I stroke the dog's warm silvery coat.
He tolerates me – enthusiasm
is kept for his sick master, whose sister and I
exchange September's ritual words
about earlier dark, about our hope
for benign autumn, shortened winter;
and feel familiar comfort,
like the gentle dog, inarticulate, warm.

I turn through the gate,
breaking a cobweb on the latch,
and focus on clasped hands, lichened words –
Jane... Edward... beloved... beloved...
Defiantly, the shutter clicks,
making its little bid to empower
a leap through solstice into light.

Recovering

You fret at unruly speech
that won't go the way you want.
You feel you're wandering
in boggy wastes, tearing yourself
on thorns of sudden thickets.
Murky night is hiding
the marker cairn.

Sometimes I want to say
"Rest now, let dark
finish your sentence".
But then I think of how
you always dominated language,
wrenched it to shapes that held
uncompromising truth. For you,
acceptance can't be passivity.
How will you contend with this
confusion of the brain's signals?
How overcome spirit's dislocation?

At the border of your harsh new land
I wait, wishing you safe road, firm tread,
starshine, reorientation

Winter Coming

At the roadside, October blackberries,
fat and red, if they ripen
will be bitter, devil-fouled.
Sun's warmth is a veil over chill.
Later, this may be a lucky autumn,
flaunting its red, gone beyond
any notion of taint or loss.
Today is too soon, today
leaves disown their touch
of dryness and tarnish, as if
hankering for summer's juice.

Winter is unclear, a dark prospect
of something to be endured.
Yet soon the tawny richness
taking over riverside trees,
upsweep of hedged fields,
last rough brown pasture before
the bare dark of mountain,
this year again will change
foreboding to anticipation.

Soon each small withering of leaf,
each miniscule hedgerow difference,
will be like a little boy
running towards us along
the empty road, calling
"It's coming! It's coming!", and we'll hear
at last, far off, drums
and, slowly growing, pulse of the dance.

November Day

Living one day at a time includes
embracing this day in November.
Clocks have gone back, the world's dipping into dark.
For a while there'll be illusory brightening
of morning, then the black slide into solstice.

Forget light that will flare from the house
Christmas-packed with returning young.
One day at a time. Forget the gleam
of sun on February's wet track,
dank ponderousness of gravid ewes.

November's your treasure, believe it,
November is now. Promises and hope
distract you from loving it, from taking
its murkiness into your arms. Let dark
wake you, delight you, and light unobserved
will creep slowly towards you, one day at a time.

Still from a TV Film

Far over all that white
the masts are so tall, so black,
and slanting, as ice holds crookedly
the two trapped ships with their unmoving sails.

The crews are gone on their long
hopeless walk into desolation, their leader
already dead, themselves doomed.

Below-deck in the empty ships, timbers
shudder in the groaning clutch of ice;
but distance makes utter stillness, utter silence.

Across relentless white the tall black shapes
soundlessly exclaim at their own
wrongness, their unnatural tilt, their ending
in this mastering, ice-mastered sea.

Morning

That morning she didn't go with him
down the stairs. She heard doors
open and close, as he looked
for anything he'd left; heard
his steps in the passage –
now he'd be lifting
his old grey coat from the nail.
The latch clicked up. For a moment
came a rush of rain, till the door
shut silence in with her again.

She had meant not to look out,
but in the low-ceilinged bedroom
the small grudging window
was too available, too near. At first
there was nothing to watch, only wet trees
hiding the downward path.
Then, up the muddy track
beyond the stream, a dwindling form
climbed to the road and was gone.

Out of a shapeless pain
came the sense that to live this,
without struggle, was all she could do
to save their yesterday.
But she stood for a long time
looking at trees blowing in rain,
taking the chilly turbulence in
to her shocked mind,
wondering what it was
that might in the end be saved.

Congregation

I despise my phobic distaste
for huge triangles of cobweb
slung from the beams.
An islet of chilly dryness
lapped by wet grass, the minute church
has been swept; the chest that serves as altar
is polished, but has no flowers.
No-one, for months and years,
can have brought a brush long enough
to reach the roof.
                         Up there
a swart indifferent congregation
of spiders has had its way,
generation after scuttering generation
spinning those filmy tents.
I wish I could find them
beautiful. I wish I could see them
as an unwilled offering wound out
from the vitals of a creature
as miraculous as any.
                         Uneasily
I glimpse above me a judder,
a twitching in a giant web, and leave,
clanging shut the door, half-heartedly attempting
some sort of valedictory acceptance
if not quite a blessing, as I wade
with leaky shoes through unmown grass.

Letters Dancing

Under this picture of script on stone
the scholars' interpretation
must be taken on trust.
I'm nowhere near
fitting meaning to shape.
The letters rock and slide,
dip, reach up –
hard to imagine them
being read as words.

This is a wild alphabet
irrepressibly dancing.
It's as if Anglesey itself –
land, sea, skies, weather –
lifted and shook it,
tilted, transformed,
set something free,
according a kingly sleeper
its own eccentric homage.

Time Being

1. The Scar

Late July is always heavy and lush.
It's more than that now –
the trees have encroached. The house
peers from a glade in the forest.
The short-cut is a bog, the gate to it
rusted, jammed shut.

I head for the old lane
to the high moors, the Black Rocks,
the waterfall I saw in winter once –
a branching frozen dazzle, weirdly silent.
But now, bafflingly, not the smallest path
leads round the hill. The track has gone.

It was a sunken lane
as far as the hill-gate.
Through gaps in flanking trees,
their leaves metallic against sun,
distances were soft, blue-dark.

Hardly need for a path – it's easy to let
the land's curve carry me on.
But there's another orientation,
weakened now, confused; to do
with children's wild screams of laughter
one soaking autumn, when the track
was a morass and sucked their boots off;
to do with years when we changed,
and the lane did not.

I suppose the trees were cut down first,
then the banks levelled, brashings tamped in
and the lot smoothed over.
                    And I suppose
I could have been standing here
centuries ago, grumbling

at the new scar of a road being clawed
out of my smooth, my perfect hill;
the rawness of it, the bristliness
of young hedge-sprouts, the tumbled earth.
I'd be unable to see the arcades
of those future trees, or feel one pulse
of the life that would course
along this channel, for a while.
                              I wouldn't know
one day I'd get my wish, the long scar healed
and the whole sweep of the hillside clear again,
answering the clarity of summer sky.

2. Amber

The year you left
your garden fought off drought
to give you its best summer.

Even in autumn,
to the last day, almost,
you brought in armfuls of roses.

A long time, twenty years,
as long as a day.

Voices overlapping in lit rooms,
laughter, rasp of crisp leaves
blown over stone.

We are held here in amber.
Coming down a half-cleared path
I find you, planting roses.

A long time, twenty years,
as long as a day, a summer, a dream.

3. Rooms

Crossing from table to window,
chair to door, isn't easy
on days when so many rooms,
superimposed, have to be traversed.
Each in its time was learnt,
its expansiveness revelled in,
its awkward narrow places
allowed for, squeezed past.

Every move brings a new set
of angles and curves, vistas,
claustrophobic corners.
Some furniture stays, re-arranged.
Some disappears, then one day
there it is, unexpectedly
blocking the way, lumping against
today's sofa, or the piano
from two houses back.
                    That piano!
It gives its music, halting, amateur
but haunting, to the room
with rose curtains. Some days
there's cacophony, one room's radio
on a high shelf shouting down
stiff-fingered scales; jingles
from a newer TV fighting them both.

Other days are simpler –
only one time and its trappings clear,
only the slightest hints and shadows
still there, too faint to matter,
easy to think memories or dreams;
a small enigmatic layering
of the stuff of things, hardly there,
hardly there at all.

4. The Pause

"A wonderful Great and unknown Creature",
wrote Traherne, waking his readers
to some idea of the strangeness
of a divine Lover.
                              Is there a sense
on this tawny silent moor with its drift of rain
glittering in stormy sun, its rainbow flung
from hill to cloud and back to autumnal earth,
of that being's elusive presence?

Nothing I see matches the map. Getting lost
here seems inevitable and good.
Till the rainbow fades, till patterns
of time and direction grow clear again,
in a stormlit pause the Creature roams the moor
and breathes with the breath of the bright rain.

Moving On

Full sun.
Running down steps into shade
where a woman is selling violets.
Buying lavishly, trying
to match the hugeness of happiness
with too many tumbling bunches
of deep soft flowers.

Dusk.
A smoky tang in the air's chill.
The time of year when lights begin
to assert a power they didn't need
in summer dark. Leaving now,
lingering under the arch
to catch the last curl of a song
round the good hours.

December dawn.
Station lights weak through mist.
Nearly time. No-one coming.
No-one else on the platform
except a man stacking boxes,
making a dull sound of slither and thump,
soon swallowed up as the train glides in.

Back

I went back
when the loved valley
was dressed in summer,
made my mind strip the land
to stark ridges of rock
in frosted grass, numbed stream
bleak as the winter sky –
and still it was home.

Others over centuries had left,
I told myself, necessity
driving some South for work, some
the few but divisive miles
downstream for easier living.
I had not thought
to be one of them, and now
felt an irrational need
to forgive myself.
                         June sun
seemed uncensorious. Today
all the valley's imagined words
were warm. I sat by the stream
and listened.

The Beach

Roadside rocks
have a moist dark sheen.
Vertical layering spells
cataclysmic wrenching, tilting,
millennia past.

Rowans cling
in crevices. This rich year
they sag with excess of berries.

Standing under
the opulent canopy,
a woman holds on her palm
a flake of stone –
embedded in it little globes,
pebbles from the beach
of a primordial sea.

Wind gets up,
loud in laden trees.
We are of no time,
or of all, as again
the ancient waters roar.

Lying About the Kite

She swears it's a red kite; he's always
wanted so much to see one.
How can she tell? – it's too far
in that cloud-bordered sky-lagoon.
"Yes," she says, lying, "yes,
I can see its forked tail."

He's leaving; the car is packed and ready,
his last holiday is over.
That elusive bird, distance shrinking it
to little more than a dot, is her chance
to give him one small thing
he's longed for.
              She's almost sure
he believes her. She's almost sure
that above whatever whirligigs
of pain he has to spin through
there'll circle, unmistakeable,
her gift, the soaring kite.

Screams

In the hills, sometimes
the car-radio couldn't speak,
sometimes it stuttered out news of war.
Spared TV pictures, we still heard
enough of horror to make the day
blood-smirched. Guilt
kept us listening.
Later, the walled garden,
that archetypal enclosure,
was beautiful as ever, but today
withheld its peace.

         And then,
across artichokes and lavender,
sweet williams and raspberries,
over the head of a girl
with barrow and spade, working
moist Carmarthenshire soil,
from wall to wall, two peacocks,
one purple-green, iridescent,
the other a fantasy of white,
began to scream.

         Unhurried,
they turned their small regal heads
towards each other, antenna-crests
trembling as they opened their beaks
and sent across the garden
harsh and terrible cries.

Whatever they were expressing was not pain,
not fear, not any human thing; yet
the ugly shrieks released
into quiet air a smothered agony
that used these violent alien voices
for proxy outcry, and could then be still.

At last the peacocks were silent.
The princely white one swung his lacy tail
in a fall of courtly flounces
down the wall, and held the pose.

Remembering Swans

The bank and ditch are all whiteness, frondiness,
still abundant, exuberant, diverse.
What would she feel? – an old woman, one day,
reaching for her out-of-date flower-book,
seeing little then in meagre hedge-rows
to match the pictures? She might mutter
a litany, "Hedge-parsley, wild carrot, chervil",
remembering delicate distinctions. She'd become
a friend to ground-elder, even, that elegant pest.

Through the gate there's a glitter and sombreness
of water – an old village reservoir, twin lakes,
tree-shaded; broken bridge; miniature dam.
Beyond, a field-path, untrodden, loses itself
on the way to the hills. A pair of swans
and five cygnets idle over the lake
to look at the stranger, and see me no threat.

One day at the water's edge an old woman
may remember how whiteness shone up
from a perfect reflection; how the cob
snaked his sleek neck down to the pen
and touched her once with his beak. Silent lake,
lifeless, lacking for years those white presences;
on the shore an old woman, remembering swans.

The Well

They dug out the well,
amazed at its depth. Friends
came to peer through the grill
at this treasure of the new home.
Frequent rain was more welcome
now it woke, far down, mysterious
responses – insistent running,
a sharper stony rattle,
sometimes in storm a plashing,
as of one body of water
spilling into another.

When the well was made,
secrets had been opened,
depths dipped into
for everyday need.
That link with man
had long been broken, yet
still the water sprang and flowed
deep in the earth.

            Some, gazing down,
longed to map channels,
understand workings, banish
all strangeness. Others heard
a language half-recognised,
and felt no need to translate.
                      Again
came rain, and those distant
enigmatic answers from something
non-human, its identity restored,
moving at its own will, alone.

Ice

I remember piprake ice
on rocks by a climbing road,
needling, stabbing the air;
and the hurt air savagely
seeking a victim, burning
my lungs with cold.
The valley seemed helpless
in an agony of white; my eyes
dazzled and ached, ears
felt a mute throbbing of pain.
Yet now in this winter's
threatening warmth, still called
'unseasonable', I could wish back
even gelid extremes, even pitiless breath
of unassailable ice at an unchanging pole.

Porch-light

Years of friendship, from childhood up –
why, seven years after her death,
this trivial memory? I can't stop thinking
of her porch-light, that would spring on
if someone came to her door in hours of dark,
or lurked, slunk nearer, passed.
                              When sometimes
it came on unexplained, it shone
unnervingly for half a minute, perhaps,
then switched off. "Only a cat or something,"
she'd say; I'd think "or something",
and not be reassured.
                        In the isolation
of my hills I had no such device;
slept soundly, ignorant of whatever
hovered, probed, slid or padded off,
maybe returned in the black night. Here
at town's edge I sensed something to fear –
and indeed there was, for her,
but no light signalled the slow approach
of that which knew her name and habitation
and would not leave without her.

Predator

The cat with a tail like a racoon
sneaks across my lawn, disappears
through rusty railings hidden in the hedge,
leaving a notion of the uncontrollable,
cruel, slithery; of dubious affinities.

What a small, comely creature on which
to unload so much mistrust! Yet surely
a predator's beauty always speaks
to our ambivalence? As he slinks by,
in my heart too a dark flower opens.

Reading a Landscape

Walking roads I half-know,
I'm reading a landscape,
searching for the word 'home'
in this new context;
some of those who found it here
touch my life and slip away.

1.

Scarcely anyone walks where the pavement ends
by the busiest road, on rough grass alongside
cars, tankers, stock-lorries, vans, four-by-fours,
and once in a while an obstructive tractor
chivvying a herd of cows. But it's from this angle
that a house whose story I've heard
can be spied sideways. Scruffy fields that flank it
hint at old parkland. A few trees
('noble', topographers might have said)
still dominate. Here and there a vestige of vista
leads the eye back to the house.
Sprouting dormer windows, stretching out
into servant's rooms, stable-yard, coach-house;
venturing on a fish-pond – here
was the modest mansion of small squires
hardly known beyond the hilly marches
of their old parishes. Later came clergy,
their style dwindling from vicar to vicar.
Now it's secular again. Always lived in,
cared for in some degree, it's never known decay,
never yielded to push and curling-in of leaves,
startle of birds in the hall. Here is only
decay's cousin a few times removed –
a just-caught shadow of loss, part
of an unfinished picture's necessary dark.

2.
On a clear day
one steep road gave a prospect
free from trick of light.
For miles the land unfolded
its flaws, beauties, logic, enigmas,
contradictions, in unemphatic
shadowless diversity, like yet unlike a map;
closer than any map could be
to those who dug, fenced, coppiced, levelled here,
bypassed, bridged, laid stone on stone,
changed and pulled down and built again.

Later next day the countryside
dissolved in grey-gold mist
of January sun. I recognised
a roadside gate, and the start of a lane
that dipped into shining haze. Years ago
I'd followed it down to a house, one of few
this loop of old road still served.
A woman farmed there, alone except
for her elegant goats, pensioned ponies,
and a tribe of wary lurchers. Unsentimentally
she helped her creatures through their lives –
at the end, she was their deft kind slaughterer.

I pictured her still there,
deep in that bowl of light,
her tall stair-window laced and swagged
with more great cobwebs than I'd ever seen.
Now little could be read
of this landscape blurred with winter sun,
I was glad of her humdrum gate, defined
where so much was vague splendour; glad
that she belonged to this place
as I might never do, glad
of the chance that before night
there could be an eddying, a firming,
someone taking shape out of dusk and mist,
a couple of lurchers all slink and snarl
running ahead of her; glad
that whether I was there or not,
this might be.

3.
On a small road that winds
up to a village in the hills,
late winter afternoon
is to be reckoned with.
It has an odd intensity,
making gate and tree exclamatory
against a livid sky.

Over a small wooden bridge
today's morass of sodden leaves
encroaches on a field. A finger-post
points blankly across it.
I think of summer, but hear, see, feel
only a winter day's dank wind, piled clouds.
I think of girls in white (how long ago?),
festive, laughing, crowding away
across the sunny field, vanishing
up a hidden valley – a puzzling image
that persists with the authority of myth:
the myth of this place? or the myth of my life,
that there's no escape from making?
Dimly-sensed seasons of the past,
an unshaped future, beat at my mind,
as now, uncertain still, in growing dark
I turn and go.

Road to the Lake

"Don't miss the road to the lake," he said,
"the cow-parsley's out" – straight away
I could see it, a small winding road
and white luxuriance
tossing in sunny wind
or stilled in a lull:
always the hope
of shining water ahead.

I didn't go. Rain came
and for days poured.
The glittering lake
slid away into dark.
               Now again
I'm making plans, searching maps
for the little road, though this time,
if I find it, there'll no longer be
those white drifts of blossom;
their time is over.
              Another year, perhaps,
another journey, and cow-parsley out
on the road to the lake.

Shape

Five years old.
An upstairs room
with a worn pink carpet
and a box of toys.
Not playing with them,
just standing by the window,
smeary with westering sun.
Fragments. A sense
of something lost.
Echoes. Longing.

Eight perhaps, or nine.
A ground-floor room.
Looking up through a narrow window
into early grey, soft rain.
At the top of steps, a pink glow –
small roses massed on an arch.
Fragments. A sense
of springing up through grey
to waking light.
Anticipation. Longing.

Old.
Trying to piece together
something never yet whole.
Trying to retrieve
beginnings; knowing endings.
Fragments. A sense
of shape, not yet clear.
Longing. A fitful hope.

Elegy

Say he caught the moment
when apples flew up
to gleam in the sky
and stars fell down
to blaze on the bough

when estuarine floods
curled back to the hill
when black never
turned to ever

say it was impossible
but he did it
say when all feeling had gone
he loved

say silence
in his song.

Destination

On the map, the Roman road
dots on, straight, as expected –
down fields, over a ford,
up a long hill.
                    On the ground,
a green lane, treebordered,
marches unswerving
the length of two fields, to a gate
where it vanishes.
                    Distantly,
the hill climbs, carrying
some sort of road; intermittently,
the beetle-shape of a car
scurries upwards.
                    Between here and there
featureless sheep-cropped grass
spreads, unhelpfully.
On what might be the Roman line,
a hedge confuses.

Down a green slope I find
a small river, and splash through –
the Roman ford? After that,
it's a squelch through rushes,
a stab of barbed wire, climbing track
almost certainly wrong,
and a remote farmhouse,
looming where least foreseen.

Heading now straight, I hope,
for the road home,
I heave open a rusty gate,
push through nettles, plunge
down the roughest of sunken lanes
into near-night; stumble and slither
out into sun, and find
                    another stream,
the stony twinkling of a ford, grace

of brushing trees. Across the water
is a small broken house
that hasn't lost its gentle air of home.
The map shows it, named and known. Once
it stood at a crossing of paths; today
there's only the nettly lane.

When plashing and scrambling have led at last
to familiar ground, looking back
I feel the day's gift was not so much
that search for the Roman road's
sharp-aimed definiteness
as the dark, chance-found lane,
lost house, young river, stooping trees –
none of it a destination planned,
none of it sure, precise, direct;
a place whose significance
was born in my mind, and has homed there;
the accidental, the unforgettable.

Firstborn

Before you were firm on your feet
you liked words. "Banister", you tried,
"mantelpiece". We wondered at your skill.
If you were quiet sometimes, and watchful,
we could almost think you waiting
to learn the name of things half-seen,
such light and strangeness your eyes had.

For a while we recaptured something
of that inclusive curiosity,
that marvelling, until
its destined fading left
you moving into our usual world
and us, having briefly borrowed yours,
trudging back now,
out of the lost lands, again.

Slide-Lecture, 'Universe'

We have seen
such deeps.

We have seen
the whole realm and system of our sun
slide into emptiness.

We have seen
two stars alone in nothingness
dance round each other.

We have seen
a vast shining galaxy
tiny, clawing at black space
with its little spiralling arms.

We have seen
such dark.

Driving home, my neighbour says
he was depressed at first, then happy to know
that there is nothing, but nothing, that matters
one jot or tittle, anywhere, anytime.
Trying to find an expressible reason
why I don't feel that, I get bogged down.

We swing round Llandovery Sugarloaf, heading north.
Soon it'll be the longest day.
Three sheep stare over the safety-rail
chewing determinedly. A lorry rockets past,
carrying a tractor. The busy-ness,
particularity of life encloses us
like an old and slightly too cosy coat,
not yet ready for recycling.

Cliffs

Suddenly far over the fields
appeared a whole sculpted hill,
white in winter sun.
                    The camera looked.
It did not see the quarry's ambivalence – its threat
to nourishing fields, to a valley's witchery;
or its promise of work, of thudding dusty life.
                    The camera looked.
Mindlessly its little screen revealed
a different reality, stranger beauty –
a vision of shining cliffs, allowed
by a kindness in the lens,
a blessing in the light.

Sea Diptych

1. Nightmare at the Film Show

Back from the Caymans, they showed
their film of a watery underworld.
Who, of however inland nature,
could not be seduced by that soft
violence of colour, frondiness, branchiness?
and the explosions of shimmering fish, their wild
wheeling and plunging, unpredictability
their art? Sudden menace –
a great shape looming, sidling by,
gone but how far, for how long? Then,
on the right of the screen,
a blind chasm. The shallow-sea shelf,
the garden of prettiness and fantasy, where grew
plushy plants, where crevices disgorged
those thousand metallic fish that seemed to play,
all fell away, down, down into dark.
Everything I'd always felt about the sea
came surging back. No editing out
of that drop could make me friend now
to such an element. Unimaginably
far down, under a drowned mountain,
in a cave as black as childhood fear, I knew
something uncurled, swivelling sightless eyes
upwards, as the film wound on
to a harmless close.

2. A Dream of Day's End

A strange end to the day – no darkness yet,
though autumn evening was drawing on;
only a pallor, a sickliness of air.
Was it possible to be sure
those were house-lights on a shore
far off, guessed more than seen,
over miles of salt-flats
and a great arm of the sea?

What certainty could there be
with mist lying grey on the marsh,
hovering pale over distant depths?
Yet what else could those tiny winkings,
those twinklings be, on the dim line
of what seemed to be land?

This was unknown country.
Imagination built over there
a town, or perhaps
a fishing-village, streets running down
to sea-front, harbour; normality
of cottages, shops, plenty of lights
hailing the coming
of ordinary dark.

But then
one by one, cluster by cluster, as though
abandoned or overwhelmed,
the little faraway lights went out.
There was only the pallid mist, thickening,
a chill in the morbid air, and questions
it might be better not to ask.

Llŵchwr

1. Thomas Jenkins at Llygad Llŵchwr
(The Eye of Loughor)

(Thomas Jenkins of Llandeilo, builder, bridge-builder and carpenter, kept a diary from 1826 to 1870. Between 1840 and 1867 he visited at intervals the cave-system in which the river Loughor rises, in the Carmarthenshire Black Mountain.)

What did it feel like, determinedly walking
into the hill, each carrying a candle?
He never tells us that. He made measurements –
*The distance from the entrance to the water
is 567 feet.* He was practical, storing body-warmth
with a brew of tea on a fire outside,
tying twine to a stalactite, for safe return.

But what did if feel like? Did candles
ever fail? Beyond their small gleams,
flickering on the asperities of rock,
the spectral stalactites, did the dark press in,
or unnervingly stretch out into – what?
Could they hear, on the left, Llŵchwr
on its way to freedom? Did they catch
an eerie whisper of water, or a booming
from those *magnificent caverns* he and his friends
floated through once, in a home-built coracle?

Believing he was first to penetrate
some of those black windings woke more
than the wish to record. Was he touched
by wonder? Here, he wrote,
man never dared go, and drew on his rough map
a *whirlpool, depth not known.* Hitting a stalactite
with his hammer made *as fine and loud a noise
as one of the largest bells in Llandeilo steeple.*

Over the years the visits grew fewer. On one,
he checked, after seven years, the stored coracle,
and found it *completely destroyed*. Twelve years later
came the last visit. He still walked right up
to the water-barrier, taking temperatures,
compass directions. Had the thrill gone?
No word to say. Whether in dreams he ever heard
a subterranean river's unearthly sound,
or the clear strong church-tower note
of the Bell Cavern stalactite, I can't know.
Yet I have the sense, illogical, inescapable,
of sharing a farewell.

2. Balancing Cat (Glynhîr Waterfall)

Only one of us seems unshaken –
the white cat, one-eared cancer-survivor,
who tight-ropes her plumply confident way
along the rail.
                Below is the frenzy
of white water. The waterfall
fills this tawny valley with its wild noise.

Pictures of the falls have spoken to the eye
in a language of swirl and spume;
today, in sun after autumn storm,
deafened, bludgeoned by savage sound,
we find this a mad place, out of control,
its beauty not kin to anything everyday –
at odds, embattled, roaring its will to destroy.

The cat has flirted with hell already,
though she didn't know it. She seems to cock
the little stump of her cancerous ear
to help the other one catch a shadow of sound;
and then sits tidily, deaf as a knob,
at the end of the rail.

3. Cup and Flow (Garden, Glynhîr)

A cup: water contained, held.
A down-rushing, clamouring whiteness: water flowing free —
two things a poet found, centuries ago.
And a third, hard to define:
behind the waterfall,
a presence.

Here the garden, quiet within walls,
is haunted by falling water, not seen, not heard
while the door in the wall is shut.
There is only breeze in the leaves,
and far-away sounds from the ancient house.
But whoever has opened the door and taken
the slithering path down through Llwchwr's ravine
to the falls, finds that the garden cups and holds
more than can be told.
                        Now there will always be
that haunting of falling water, wild in storm
or soft in the quiet seasons;
power that can't be shut out
by walls and doors of the mind.

Then and now
the cup:
the endless fall:
the haunting.

Film, 'Gwesyn'

"As if we were there," the film-makers
wanted us to feel. Pictures caught
the undulations of moorland heights,
the dip and dip of folded valleys,
plunge and swirl of the stream we traced,
tiny beauties of unexpectedly
exotic flowers. Always hills reached away
into a summoning distance.

                    Recorded sound
beat us with lonely relentless wind,
enveloped us with the young river's roar,
or else in quiet let us hear
raven and lark. Indeed
I was there again, back where for years
the plod and scramble miles upstream,
the tussocky trudge on the plateau above,
had seemed too difficult; and to forget
or remember, a choice of regrets.

Knowing again, vicariously,
the concentrated life of my
irreplaceable solitudes, I felt
it mattered little to be there
or far away, young or old, even
alive or dead, as long as that
uncompromising beauty stayed.
Over bogland and rock of life there shone
that realisation, like a brief sweep of sun
caught by the camera and saved, between
vast chilly surges of the clouds.

Falconer

They say he kept a pet fox,
old Morgan the Falconer,
His barn is still here, below the track,
but where's the house?
This isn't only something found in deeds,
named in old wills; it's a memory, too,
of my own – the children leaning
from a window bare of glass, the man
standing in a derelict garden.

Go back a century, and half of another.
Find Morgan here. One falcon
lived in the house. She was quiet enough
when he was near to steady her;
she'd have no truck with his wife.
Claws gripping her rail, she'd stare,
unhooded, with eyes of the wild. The rest,
savage beauties caught to be sold,
native to cliffs by the Pembrokeshire sea,
led their darkened lives caged in the barn,
except when the falconer gave them sight
and flung them each in turn at the sky,
till hunger enticed it down.

So often there comes a hope
to see what was seen, go a tiny step
towards understanding, feel more oneness
than separation. Then failure again –
too many changes, too daunting difference.
Patience, patience. Wait. Keep a steady watch.
Out of a turbulent sky, something
riding the gusts of this wind
at the edge of autumn
will stoop to the lure.

Pelican Vulning

The pelican is vulning her breast.
The painter has shown
a delicate spray of blood
springing forth towards the chick,
who looks pleased, even mildly
excited, though unsurprised.
She obviously deems maternal vulning
no more than her due, a very proper
recognition of needs and duties.

Neither bird looks much like a pelican,
being of slim build, freckle-feathered
and pointy-beaked.
"Possibly Chinese influence",
we learn, and reserve judgement
on the freckliness and daintiness
of Chinese pelicans.
        It is, anyway,
a charming picture, the elegant mother
with looping neck and stabbing beak, the chick
cheerfully hopping with half-raised wings
to receive her feast.
        What, after all,
she may be anthropomorphically thinking,
is a mother for?

Acknowledgements

Acknowledgements are due to the editors of the following magazines where some of these poems first appeared: *Cambria, The Interpreter's House, Planet, Poetry Scotland, Poetry Wales, Quattrocento, Roundyhouse, Scintilla;* also to the Cinnamon Press anthology, *The Lie of the Land*.

'Cart-Burial, Young Adult Female' was a first prize winner in *Roundyhouse* and the title sequence, 'Time Being', in *Scintilla*.

I should also like to acknowledge the encouragement and valued judgement, over the years, of my poetry editor, Amy Wack.